100 PROMPTS

for SCIENCE FICTION WRITERS

100 PROMPTS
for SCIENCE FICTION WRITERS

LESLIE AND JAROD ANDERSON

STERLING
New York

STERLING
New York

An Imprint of Sterling Publishing
387 Park Avenue South
New York, NY 10016

STERLING and the distinctive Sterling logo are registered trademarks
of Sterling Publishing Co., Inc.

© 2014 by Jarod Anderson and Leslie Anderson

2-3 & throughout, 42, 59, 72: © sdecoret/iStock; 28: © Filatov Alrxey/
Shutterstock; 88: © 1971yes/iStock; 105: © oorka/iStock

All rights reserved. No part of this publication may be reproduced,
stored in a retrieval system, or transmitted in any form or by any means
(including electronic, mechanical, photocopying, recording, or otherwise)
without prior written permission from the publisher.

ISBN 978-1-4549-1429-7

Distributed in Canada by Sterling Publishing
c/o Canadian Manda Group, 165 Dufferin Street
Toronto, Ontario, Canada M6K 3H6
Distributed in the United Kingdom by GMC Distribution Services
Castle Place, 166 High Street, Lewes, East Sussex, England BN7 1XU
Distributed in Australia by Capricorn Link (Australia) Pty. Ltd.
P.O. Box 704, Windsor, NSW 2756, Australia

For information about custom editions, special sales, and premium
and corporate purchases, please contact Sterling Special Sales at
800-805-5489 or specialsales@sterlingpublishing.com.

Manufactured in the United States of America

2 4 6 8 10 9 7 5 3 1

www.sterlingpublishing.com

CONTENTS

INTRODUCTION

Science Fiction (SF), like many of its characters, tends to be born in a laboratory. It also tends to live right on the edge of human knowledge and understanding. The idea for a SF story often grows out of a scientific principle, a strange application of technology, a new discovery, or a gap in our knowledge about the universe. SF, however bizarre, is anchored to our reality, its laws, and its consequences. It is often considered a sibling to Fantasy, as both have elements of the fantastical and unbelievable, but SF is very much its own, unique genre.

All SF has some fantastic elements: rocket ships, unearthly diseases, giant fighting robots, etc. What differentiates SF from Fantasy is that Fantasy's unusual elements are born of imagination. There is no need for dragons, magic, and unicorns to have any tangible connection to the "real world." On the other hand, SF's fantastical elements are built upon a premise of reality. Regardless of whether a SF story explores the ramifications of a new technology or describes the first contact between aliens and humanity, the plot typically wears an air of plausibility. This connection to reality gives SF its punch. Couching the unlikely within the solidly real gives SF the power of "what if," making the impossible seem, well, possible.

These prompts, carefully grown and tended in our labs before being set loose on an unsuspecting world, are a first step. They are a laboratory door left slightly ajar, an invitation into possible worlds. However, the best SF has the same building blocks as all great literature: an immersive, engaging story and strong, well-developed, empathetic characters. Although flying cars or a supercomputer bent on world domination might be at the center of your story, the thing that makes us remember it, and love it, is the emotional connection between the reader and the characters who populate your strange world. For that reason, we tried to focus many of the questions that are paired with the prompts on a character, rather than the larger world or context.

What does your character want? What is he willing to do to achieve it? What challenges does he face? Whom or what does he care about?

Subgenres within Science Fiction are tricky, and there are, no doubt, many alternative systems of categorization to the one presented in this book. The subgenre tags we employed here have been selected because they are consistently represented in SF publishing. In other words, these are the tropes and themes that helped build SF and that show up again and again. The prompts in this book have been sorted into seven categories: The Pulp, Interstellar, Biological, Aftermath, Futurescapes, Tech, and Another Time. These subgenres are not meant to be restrictive, and, indeed, many of the prompts presented in this book fit into more than one category. Feel free to combine subgenres or to move freely between them, mixing elements from each. Would you like your Biological story to happen in outer space? Mix in some elements from Interstellar. With laser guns? Sprinkle in some Pulp. It's up to you! If you are interested in publishing your work, subgenre distinctions can help you send your story to the most appropriate market or editor.

While exploring the prompts in this book, remember that the questions are there to guide you, but you need not answer all of them—or any of them, even. Remember that challenging the characters and testing the logic of your plot makes for unexpected, interesting narratives. Although these prompts are specific, every story produced from them will be unique, because each writer will create distinctive characters, challenges, and nuances. These story ideas are a fun way to challenge your craft and grow your skill as a writer. 🌐

The PULP

SPACE OPERA,
CAMPY,
SENSATIONAL

An alien race of winged superbeings has emerged from a tear in space-time and taken control of early-twentieth-century Earth. Vicious and organized, they quickly crushed our surprised defenses and seized control of humanity's technology. Now, with the help of a very unusual scientist, a group of underground freedom fighters has a new weapon that just might turn the tide of battle. The jetpack.

A jetpack and an electro-sword aren't much, but they'll get you to one of the enemy's hoverbases and give you the element of surprise. Will that be enough? Your move.

A spaceship is eaten by a massive space-worm! As the crew travels through the monster, they find ships from a wide variety of times and places, long since crashed and dead. Finally they come across a society living inside the space-worm. The citizens of this society are generations removed from their crash-survivor ancestors and refuse to believe they are inside a creature.

How would this society greet outsiders? Would the crew want to convince them of the truth? Will the crew escape or assimilate?

Psychic/telekinetic mimes terrorize civilians by holding them for ransom in invisible boxes. The city's only hope is in a rogue mime who was dismissed from the evil crew for speaking a single word.

What was the word? How will the mime overpower the superior numbers of his former gang?

A waiter in an interstellar café overhears a plot to assassinate the Space President. He wants to intervene, but he can't leave the café. He can only try to influence the action through the diners.

Why can't he leave the café? What can he say to influence patrons? What happens if he says the wrong thing?

As humanity expands into the stars, it becomes more and more difficult to deliver a simple message or a package. A species of aliens, generally more adaptable to different atmospheres and environments, sets up a galactic post office. Most governments consider them above conflict, and they're given safe passage (with inspections) through the most disputed areas of space.

Does the post office begin to use its power for evil? For good? Can they be bought by one side in a conflict? How might a single post office worker react when they are asked to spy or deliver a secret message? What would be the price of the post office losing its neutrality?

A mad scientist obsessed with Greek mythology sets out to make mythical monsters a reality through genetic engineering. A scientist with the same obsession sets out to stop him by creating legendary heroes. What drives these characters to battle? What drives their obsessions with myths? Does this dynamic cause them to feed each other's insanity?

cience has not developed a way to stop the body from dying and decaying, but it can remove people's brains and reinstall them in robot bodies built to their specifications!

What kind of bodies would people choose? Would they want to look nearly human or be strange and unique? How do human interactions change if someone's uncle decides to be a giant mechanical centipede?

It takes a lot of technology to get someone to the moon, but once the rockets leave the outlaws rule. A civilized, cosmopolitan Earthling is forced to move to a lawless moon-town because of economic catastrophe. He discovers a place that seems old-fashioned in brutality. For example, hangings take longer on the moon because there's less gravity, but there are still plenty of horse thieves.

How does our hero handle this futuristic Wild West?

Our hero wakes up and immediately notices that his left hand is now a tentacle. He has a vague suspicion that this has to do with his recent past (something he took at the club, his risky job at the chemical plant, or perhaps the dare he took to touch that . . . whatever it was).

Does he see this as a blessing or a curse? Does he reveal this to anyone? Is this the end of his transformation or just the beginning?

I n an effort to make interstellar travel more economically feasible, a new technology is developed that places people in suspended animation and then shoots them, bullet-like, to their destination in small, shielded pods. The technology works perfectly, until some pods fail to reach their destinations. Soon after, the shattered wreckage of a pod arrives with the remains of a strange tentacle still clinging to its surface. Deep in interstellar space, something is hunting the pods.

Will people abandon the cheaper tech because of this revelation? Will they fight back against the strange predators? Will someone volunteer as bait for the space squids?

Small, one-man rocket ships, designed like gravity-resistant motorcycles, become almost instantly popular with gangs. They can now move their turf wars into space. The fights are violent and deadly. The government is concerned that these fights will increasingly endanger civilian ships.

What can the government do to control the violence? Why are these fights important to the gangs? Why would they endanger civilians?

Scientists on a space station have assigned everyone a new, highly intelligent, talking animal to help with their jobs! They did not account for neurological and social differences between humans and animals, which results in very disruptive habits. Cats are incurably honest, hamsters terribly ADD, and dogs have trouble leaving one task for another.

What problems might this cause? How will one person, dealing with a highly sensitive task, deal with his strange animal companion?

Technology has been created to maintain Earth's atmosphere and temperature regardless of its position in space. The Earth is fitted with a propulsion system that draws on the planet's own internal heat. No longer dependent on the sun, the Earthlings decide to set sail for a new galactic neighborhood.

Who drives the Earth? How do they decide where to stay? What are the new neighbors like?

Dolphins and whales are smarter than we thought. Much smarter. Aquatic mammals have begun to band together to form their own societal infrastructures and technology. Pretty impressive for creatures without thumbs. Now they are fighting back against human encroachment and claiming the resources of the oceans as their own. Some humans advocate all out battle to take back the seas. Others advocate communication and diplomacy.

What are the ethical dilemmas in determining who "owns" the ocean's resources? Does might make right in the fight for oceanic dominance? Were whales and dolphins always this smart, or does this change indicate a strange, new, outside influence?

A seemingly empty spaceship docks at a space station. The crew of the station is confused, but, before long life begins to return to normal. One day the head of the station goes missing and a ransom note is found stabbed to the main console with a shuriken. Space ninjas! Our hero is the head of security at the space station.

How does someone fight space ninjas? Will the old pop culture archives in the computer be of any help? Can the solution be found in cheesy old ninja movies?

Psychically sensitive aliens show up and complain that Earth is being too loud. They are obviously more technologically advanced than us and more than a little intimidating.

What is the discussion on Earth? Do we meet their demands and try to be more "neighborly?" What major changes would have to happen in society? Are Zen Buddhists recruited to help quiet noisy minds? Do people fight back to retain their freedom of thought? What are the consequences if Earth doesn't quiet down?

Large animals, like cows, horses, and elephants, are proving impossible to transport in space. They quickly panic in small spaces and can cause damage to the intricate ships. So a breathing apparatus and jet pack is fashioned for the large animals, allowing them fairly free movement through space, and shepherds are hired to coax the animals from one planet to the next.

What sort of person would become a space shepherd? What are some problems they might encounter? Are there wolves between the stars?

INTERSTELLAR

ALIENS, OTHER WORLDS, SPACE TRAVEL

Two civilizations separated by millions of light-years have developed a vital, symbiotic relationship with one another over many generations. This relationship is made possible by a wormhole in space that allows for relatively easy travel between the two planets. The populations of both worlds have become completely integrated with one another. Now, the wormhole is becoming unstable, and travel between the two worlds may soon be impossible.

What difficult choices would need to be made by a resident of one of the planets with friends, family, and financial interests spread across both worlds? Can each world survive without the other? How far will they be willing to go to reconnect the planets?

liens arrive on Earth as refugees from war or famine. There are a significant number of them, and caring for them requires a great deal of resources and space. They insist that they can't go back where they came from and that Earth is their only hope.

What sociopolitical/economic/religious fallout would occur from the sudden arrival of space refugees and their long-term habitation of Earth?

T. wo alien species discover they can inter-breed. The couples and their offspring face prejudice and opposition from "purist" holdouts. Just as the Purists gain political clout one of their leaders has an interspecies child.

What is the social fallout from this event? How does the larger political narrative intertwine with the personal struggle of the disgraced Purist family? Do they learn tolerance and acceptance or hold onto their hate?

The average citizen has access to space travel, creating an Old West-style approach to land claims in the galaxy. New laws will soon change all that. Space travel, land, and salvage rights will be much more limited. These laws take effect in thirty days. There is a scramble to claim as much as possible before then.

Who are the winners and losers in this arrangement? Who holds power, and who has the advantage? What are people willing to risk and sacrifice in order to claim something for themselves?

crew is sent to a planet with no way to return. The time required for interstellar travel means that the ship is equipped with supplies for generations. One colony has developed the ability to travel faster and wants to visit the other colonies.

Will these groups still have anything in common? Will the visitors be welcomed? What could be gained by such a meeting? What might be lost?

Humans discover a planet that seems very much like Earth. The first colony does well, and people begin to settle there, many bringing pets and livestock. The animals hate it. In fact, most of them panic until they pass out or even die from long-term stress.

What spiritual or superstitious explanations might crop up for the phenomenon? How far will people go to protect their animals? What is the source of the animals' panic?

In order to excite nervous tourists about space travel, the government has hired several semi-famous artists to spend several months in space and paint the sights. They are given the run of the ships that will one day carry tourists through the stars. One painter chooses a small planetoid of brilliant color and begins to paint images of it day after day. He soon begins to suspect that the planet may not be a planet at all—that it is beginning to move, that it might be trying to communicate with him.

What would be the challenges of space-art? How would our expectations of visual art change? What would someone do it they were faced with a dangerous, but fascinating creature? Would the artist want to communicate? Is it all in his head?

Aliens conquer Earth, but make very few changes to the way people live. Apparently the symbolic ownership of a planet is what's important to them, and they have done this with several other planets.

Would humans tolerate being owned if it's purely symbolic? How would people rebel if there are very few rules to rebel against?

An astronaut, or group of astronauts, goes on a mission knowing that they will never come back. Their ship will leave the known galaxy and spiral into space.

What do they find out there? How does a scientist deal with new, amazing information when they can't communicate it back to Earth? How will the relationships between astronauts change when chain-of-command no longer matters?

Matter can be transformed into energy and remade into matter by receivers aboard interstellar ships. People and things can be transported across space. Unfortunately, during a time of great conflict and panic, the transporter-equipped ships had to be abandoned and society lost track of the positions of the receiver-ships in space. Exploration teams are needed to brave wherever the receivers may be and discover the locations. Once they're sent into space as energy transmissions, it's unclear where they will go or if they will arrive at all.

Who would accept this possibly suicidal mission? What type of team would be best to take on this mission?

Visitors from another galaxy bring Earth new perspectives and new technology. Unfortunately, human physiology makes us too fragile for light-speed travel, so the alien visitors agree to act as humanity's emissaries to other worlds. The visitors promise to establish new trade agreements and alliances. Everything seems to be going well, but once the visitors have made themselves indispensable, they begin demanding increasingly strange things in exchange for their continued help. Our hero is a young entrepreneur taking advantage of the new galactic trade routes. Unhappy with the visitors' new demands, she seeks to cut them out of the deal.

How can she do this? Will there be any retribution from the alien middlemen?

Interstellar transports have become the new subway of the twenty-seventh century. Tired commuters, wanderers, and panhandlers all huddle into the new technology each morning, trying not to spill space-coffee on each other. When a catastrophic technical failure shuts down the public transport systems, people find themselves stuck on Earth. People used to daily interstellar travel feel trapped and claustrophobic on their home planet.

How will people handle the cabin fever? What if the transports never start running again?

A lien parasites arrive on Earth and infect humans. The parasites are of human or greater intelligence and a dialogue is opened to negotiate the terms of um . . . occupation. While the negotiations are underway, there is a ceasefire between the two species, so those infected with the parasites must find a way to carry on with their daily lives.

What if some people don't follow the ceasefire? How might our hero handle something sentient living in his body? What do people do to try to get rid of the parasites on their own?

BIOLOGICAL

BIOTECH,
MICROBIOLOGICAL,
GENETIC
ENGINEERING,
SUPERPOWERS

The rise of neural implants means the end of a whole host of diseases, ranging from depression to dementia. The manufacturers of the implants launch an extensive public relations campaign focused on these medical miracles. However, there are rumors of very wealthy and well-connected individuals purchasing implants to increase their intelligence, and some speak of devices with much stranger applications and abilities. A low-level employee at a neural implant manufacturer has seen something she shouldn't have.

Should she quit? Tell the press? Blackmail the company? Or would she become obsessed with gaining the power she has witnessed for herself?

Through genetic modification, people gain the ability to photosynthesize. It's cheap, easy, and sold as a cure for global hunger and obesity!

How are resources reallocated now that humanity needs to produce much less food? What political and economic conflicts arise when people are much more self-sufficient? Would anyone refuse to participate? Why?

The government begins altering existing animals to fight a specific threat, either manmade or extraterrestrial. For example, scientists might alter killer whales to battle aquatic alien invaders. This includes making them highly intelligent, which creates its own problems.

What happens when/if these engineered animals defeat the threat they were designed to fight? What if they decide not to fight at all?

Secretly, a private lab develops the ability to stop the aging process. Before moving forward, they test the procedure on five couples. Biologically, it works perfectly, but after observing the couples in the real world for several years the project is scrapped entirely.

What did the scientists observe that convinced them to stop? What would happen to a person if they never aged? Would they be more cautious, knowing that death was not a foregone conclusion, or would they feel invincible? Would they try to insulate themselves, or make long-term plans to change the world? What happens to the ageless couples?

The crew of a ship of scientists tracks interstellar viruses that attack planets the way biological viruses attack cells. These viruses are not wholly understood, but the crew comes to suspect that they may be sentient.

Will the crew try to communicate with the viruses? Will their discovery affect their mission to destroy them?

A covert government agency is tasked with spying on a notorious warlord/dictator. All attempts at infiltrating the warlord's operations have failed, but one piece of information has been uncovered: the warlord has a personal zoo and is a prodigious collector of exotic animals. After our hero's partner is killed by the warlord, he volunteers for an experimental procedure in which his consciousness is transferred into a gorilla. One government–orchestrated, black-market sale later, our hero finds himself inside the warlord's zoo.

What now? Do the other animals smell an imposter? Will our hero have the opportunity to take out the warlord? Will he ever be human again?

The bees have all died out. Facing the prospect of crops failing and a starving population, huge numbers of Earth's citizens are called upon to act as surrogate pollinators until a solution can be found. CEOs, bankers, engineers, waiters, men, women, and children all find themselves side by side, cotton swabs in hand, doing the job bees once did for us—spreading pollen from one plant to another.

What is the cultural impact of the sudden "all hands on deck" approach to life and death ecology? What if a solution is found? Will the experience change human society in any significant way?

As a solution to population growth and over-crowding on Earth, scientists devise a way to alter human physiology to allow for life under the sea. Once the genetic procedure is complete, the individual and their offspring will no longer be able to survive on land without an air-breathing apparatus.

What are the new challenges faced by these underwater pioneers? What's their relationship like with the humans on land? Given that the planet is two-thirds water, is it possible the ocean nations would become more powerful than the land nations?

Scientists work to engineer a plant that will grow aggressively in inhospitable and extreme climates. The goal was innocent, to help regrow mountainsides in danger of mud-slides. One sample grows too well, and almost overnight, the scientists lose control. The plant moves across the Midwest, overgrowing cities and towns. Eventually people accept that this is simply something they will have to learn to live with.

What changes will people have to make to their daily schedules? Are there any advantages to the plants? What are some major disadvantages?

H umans have colonized a very harsh planet. The geography is unforgiving, hot, and mostly desert or mountain ranges. There is one place where humans have built a mostly safe home—a small jungle nestled in a mountain valley. There are a number of strange plants in the jungle whose phosphorescence attracts small animals and then the plant catches and digests them. Recently, the colonists have begun to suspect the plants are luring humans, especially children, hypnotizing them, and coaxing them close enough to eat.

How will the humans deal with the plants? Will eliminating them change the ecosystem? If they leave the jungle what challenges will they face?

On a global scale, humans start to be born without the ability to produce a certain vital amino acid, a mutation that can prove debilitating or fatal. The population is devastated before a biochemical manufacturer discovers a solution. The manufacturer uses this leverage over the human race to gain political power over the remaining population, setting up a quasi-feudal society.

How does an individual rebel if he or she needs a daily pill to survive?

№ 42

An alien spaceship crashes in the middle of Antarctica. Investigations suggest that the ship was some kind of ark, carrying multiple species of animals. One species escapes and begins to thrive in the Antarctic climate. Some argue in favor of eradicating the species, while others argue that it should be integrated into its new ecosystem.

What are the consequences? What are the benefits? As a researcher tasked with investigating this species, what are the ethical and practical questions that must be answered?

Using a clandestine custom-made virus to introduce foreign DNA into unsuspecting people, a pharmaceutical company is secretly creating a market for its own line of genetic medicines. An epidemiologist begins to suspect foul play because of the uniform distribution of the specific disease.

Where does his research lead him? How far is he willing to go to expose the criminal act of the company?

A planet very similar to Earth is found relatively nearby. Based on temperature stability and the presence of liquid water, colonization seems like an appealing option. Unfortunately, the planet's atmosphere has far more carbon dioxide than Earth's atmosphere. Searching for a solution, scientists realize that it would be easier to change the physiology of human beings than to change the atmosphere of the planet. The technology exists to modify lungs to breathe carbon dioxide rather than oxygen.

Is anyone willing to undergo the procedure in order to colonize the new world? Is the process reversible? Would colonists ever be able to return to Earth?

Humanity becomes aware of a new species of fish the size of an aircraft carrier. A small school of the colossal animals have, apparently, remained hidden in the deepest parts of the ocean for centuries. Now they're on the move, heading to warmer or colder climates.

What has caused these creatures to move? How would countries or individuals react to this discovery? Would humanity be frightened by these creatures? Would they approach them?

A group of five people is injected with a serum to give them superpowers. Based on animal testing, the injection was thought to be safe. However, now in human subjects, the serum develops rapid carcinogenic qualities and begins quickly killing the human test subjects.

Faced with their own rapidly approaching deaths, how do these new superbeings use their powers?

AFTER-MATH

**DISASTER,
POST-APOCALYPTIC**

Nº 47

Long ago humanity had hundreds of settlements around the galaxy. These settlements often had huge greenhouse space stations to produce oxygen. Now, humanity is declining, and most of the untended greenhouse stations are overrun by the forests that once kept humanity alive. One such station becomes the last safe haven for a ship of human refugees. They must carve out a pioneer life on the overgrown station.

What challenges would these people face? What other life might have survived and thrived on the abandoned station?

ecause of devastating air pollution, society moves underground. Everyone is registered and tracked carefully, because of the limited resources. That is, except for the few who aren't registered. A small group live off the grid. One day, a stranger shows up and wants to join them.

Does the group trust this stranger? What are the consequences of letting him join? Why would he want to go off the grid?

Alien tech is sent to conquer Earth. It was built to fight in open spaces and is easily confused by complex, interior areas. Mankind responds by building huge, labyrinthine cities, full of secret passages and tight corridors. Generations later, there is no sign of the aliens, but no one knows if it's safe to leave the giant mazelike settlements.

Would an individual decide to leave, or would it be a group decision? What would the consequences be of breaking the system? How does one prepare to leave the maze?

№ 50

A futuristic, self-sustaining prison colony receives news that a contagion has ravaged the outside world. In fact, the survivors must turn to the isolated colony for help.

Do the prisoners help the society that shunned them? What arrangement might be made? Who negotiates? Do they even have the ability to let others into the prison?

№ 51

A contagion sweeps through a small, isolated country. The virus takes a few hundred lives, mostly the elderly. It also renders nearly the entire population mute. Now the average citizen must learn to communicate and carry out their everyday lives in silence, while the government must decide if they can remain isolated or ask for outside help.

What types of communication would now become important? What would a society lose with spoken language? What might it gain in the quiet?

№ 52

Singularity has been accomplished. Humanity has been uploaded into a singular consciousness and no longer needs physical forms. However, a minority has been found to be incompatible with the singularity and have been left behind on Earth.

How does this group of people reconstruct society? How does this affect their view of themselves or of their group? What rules will they change? What will they want to keep?

A wannabe supervillain blows up the moon. Nobody thought he was actually dangerous, but he somehow managed to pull off his evil plot. The villain is quickly captured and thrown in jail, but now there are other problems to worry about. Among other things, the destruction of the moon affects the tides and the stability of the Earth's orbit.

How does humanity approach this new normal? Can an artificial moon be created? If so, how, and what sacrifices would people be willing to make?

Advances in medical science make people effectively immortal. These advances paired with widespread resistance to population control means Earth's ability to feed its population is taxed to the breaking point. The few immortals ruthless and cunning enough to survive the resulting collapse wander the wasteland, fighting for resources. The following generations do not have access to the advanced tech of the past and are much weaker and short lived.

Do the immortals treat the new generations as family or burdens and subjects? Can the younger generations fight back?

No one living remembers the war against the robots. Complex technologies are a specter of humanity's ancient past. Most people live a quiet, agrarian lifestyle. Our hero is a brilliant misfit whose natural curiosity has made her a pariah among her own people. Exploring a hillside near her village, she finds the remains of an underground robotics lab. When she tries to tell her people of the wonders she's discovered, she is driven away as a "witch." Taking up residence in the old lab, she decides to see just how much "witchcraft" she can learn.

How does our hero cope with her new isolation? Does she create inventions to benefit humanity or take revenge? Does anyone go looking for her?

s the Earth becomes more acidic and the air becomes harder to breathe, the wealthy build homes on tall, thin supports miles above the surface. Those who live below tell stories of these palaces, populated by robot servants and flying cars. Suddenly, the wealthy leave the planet, in a mass exodus to new, high-tech space stations. The tall cities are left to rust and collapse onto those below. Our hero has decided to investigate one of these lofty refuges and see what secrets are still inside.

What does he find? What dangers does he have to face? What does he bring back?

arth has been conquered. People have come to terms with living under our unassailable alien overlords. It could be better. It could be worse. Humans are settling into their lives in beige, cubicle drudgery. When our hero receives a clandestine post-it-note with talk of revolution, he must weigh improving his bland life against an unimaginably hideous death at the hands of the office death-bot.

What does he choose? What is at stake? Does he involve anyone else? Why did they choose him? What motivation would he have to maintain the status quo, or break it?

The country is at peace. The affluent spend most of their time and attention making their lives fun, building flying machines, toys, and developing various recreational drugs. When a neighboring country invades, a great deal of the luxury items are confiscated to help fill the gaps in the country's military readiness. The idle wealthy find themselves suddenly drafted into combat. This change results in a lot of culture shock very quickly.

How will the affluent citizens and the military mix? How will they navigate violence and danger? What will the experiences mean for postwar society?

FUTURE-SCAPES

FUTURE SOCIETIES, DYSTOPIAS

№ 59

In the future, violent wars rage. However, they're mostly proxy wars fought digitally. These proxy wars are waged by computers, but have actual, tangible geopolitical consequences in the real world.

Who runs these computers? What effects do they have on the real world? What happens if someone suggests simply turning them off?

№
60

In order to save our world, aliens who have been secretly monitoring us transport the entire planet into orbit around a star similar to our sun. They give humanity a terse explanation of why it was necessary and then disappear again. The aliens' intentions seem benign, but the lack of communication (or inability to communicate) makes them seem suspicious, or even terrifying, to most people.

Why would an alien race save humanity from a calamity? If there were no calamity, why would the aliens put in so much effort? Does an outside influence making decisions for humanity finally unite the species or further divide it?

N⁰ 61

As population explodes around the world, cities continue to grow upward, farther and farther into the skies. The wealthier citizens are able to live near to the top, while the poorest live far below, in the dark. The city's foundations are starting to break, and those at the bottom are beginning to notice.

How will they get the attention of those who can stop the decay? Are they willing to risk themselves to save the city above, or do they venture into the strange, open countryside?

War is an ugly artifact of humanity's distant past. Violence has become unthinkable to the average citizen. Conflicts are solved via complex negotiation protocols carried out by computers—everything from border disputes between nations to arguments over who will pay the bar tab. So, when a cache of cryogenically frozen scientists is discovered deep in a forgotten undersea laboratory, they struggle to assimilate into a world they find both fascinating and alien.

What happens if some of the scientists decide to reintroduce violence into the world? Who will stop them? Will violence be necessary to stop violence?

ncredible advances in transportation make it cheap and easy to get anywhere on the planet in a matter of minutes. A short walk and a five-minute ride will get you to any city in the world for practically nothing. Jobseekers can easily look for work anywhere in the world. There's no such thing as a "long distance relationship." And there's no excuse for losing touch with friends and family.

What does it mean for society that an individual's identity, education, job prospects, and personal network is no longer tied to a specific locality? Does this technology make the world feel smaller or are the possibilities overwhelming? What does it mean when it's harder to cut ties?

The government monitors marriages based on genetics. If the chance of mutation in future children is too high, the couple is not allowed to procreate.

What happens to a couple applying for marriage if one of them very much wants to have a child? What happens if one of these couples accidentally or purposefully has a child outside the government-imposed structures? How does that child fit into a society that believes it shouldn't exist?

Through robotic automation society has achieved a utopia. Citizens of the planet have been freed from daily work and most suffering or want. With no resource scarcity, warfare has ended.

Assuming that overcoming conflict, struggle, and challenge are part of the formula for human happiness and fulfillment, how does this new society provide that?

Our dimension collides with another. Transdimensional interactions create duel worlds, transposed one on top of the other. People find that they can step between the dimensions at will. This creates a lot of new real estate and resources as well as some fascinating complications. Governments move to quickly regulate movement between dimensions to buy time to understand what's happening.

What stopgap rules do they make? How and why do people oppose them?

Starvation is a thing of the past, but real food is a luxury only the very wealthy can afford. The vast majority of Earth's population gets their nutrition via pill or injection. Farms and farmers now cater only to very rich clients who can afford to subsidize the old, inefficient means of food production. One farmer, however, has decided that natural food and food production is a human birthright and sets out on a one-man quest to teach a tech-savvy populous the rewards of gardening and actual eating.

Is anyone interested in the old ways of food production? Is there any pushback from wealthy farmers who don't want to let the "trade secrets" out of the bag?

Advances in medical science mean that nearly any wound can be quickly and easily healed. The technology is so effective and widely available that most citizens have in their pockets the ability to essentially bring back the recent dead or dying. Because of these advances, some groups (especially among the teenaged population) are making a game of violence, having duels with real swords and guns, crashing cars for fun, etc. Our hero is a young police officer.

What does it mean for law and society that violence can be so easily undone? What are the nonphysical effects of such violence? Does this new technology change the law and police procedures?

A single political power has been in charge for as long as anyone can remember. One key to their continued success is that they create ways for people to rebel, scheduling protests and movements against themselves, so that they can still appear abused and harassed. One person discovers this tactic and begins a rebellion against the rebellion.

Why do they want to challenge the reigning political party? What weakness does the party have that our hero can exploit? Who is the face of this political party? Who are its agents?

A pragmatically minded society creates a super-durable material, making it possible to construct items that last a lifetime. People rarely need to shop, and money is mostly exchanged for perishable items like food and medicine.

How would this change a society that was once based on consumerism? Would people still treasure ephemeral things? Would they treasure them more or less?

F acial recognition software and constant surveillance are the norm. The civilization is used to being watched at all times. However, a small group of hoodlums discovers that certain makeup—very dramatic and dark—confuses the cameras. They experiment and learn a great deal about what types of makeup produce results. More serious and dangerous organized crime families become interested in the gang and recruit them, by force or persuasion, to disguise their members.

Is the gang willing to go along? Are they excited to be involved in bigger things, or do they miss their low-level crime? Who can they turn to for help?

№
72

Military robots secure a country long abandoned by humans. In the ruins, the robots that once served people as butlers, sales-bots, and so forth hide from the warrior-bots who guard the empty world. One day, one of the service-bots finds an infant.

How do these robots view humanity? What do they think of the programming that makes them human-analogs? Do they feel liberated, lost, or something else? Do all the robots agree on what to do with the baby?

eople are spending more and more time in virtual reality, both for education and entertainment. Many see the technology as a blessing, yet it's becoming harder and harder to ignore the fact that almost everyone who dies after prolonged interaction with virtual reality lingers in the virtual space. The government insists they're not ghosts, but what else could they be?

What do the ghosts want? What beliefs conflict with the existence of the ghosts? How would people try to interact with them?

TECH

CYBERPUNK, COMPUTERS, ROBOTICS

The government develops nanobots that can steal memories. They can be used to remove traumatic memories from entire communities or nations. This must go hand-in-hand with cleansing visual and physical evidence, of course.

What would happen if a single person were unaffected? What if someone discovered evidence of a memory they no longer had? How could an individual act on their conspiracy theory?

ighly Intelligent robots are used for most tasks—from cleaning to construction to business operations. A society begins to develop among the robots, including prejudices, expectations, and class systems. As humans struggle to understand these changes in their creations, robots realize their beliefs and practices echo their creators.

How do the robots react to this revelation? Do any robots rebel against this status quo? Would humans encourage this behavior or reject it?

cientists create a device that can remove experiences and talents from one person and place them in another. If a person is convicted of a crime, dies, or simply chooses to, their experiences can be removed and given to someone else. These experiences are enormously expensive, but there is a lottery that normal citizens can enter to win valuable experience. Our hero needs to win that lottery.

Why does the hero need the experience? What are the moral implications of taking something someone else earned? What unexpected mental symptoms might come with taking on another person's experiences?

Nº 77

Quantum computers, capable of breaking any code, make encryption a thing of the past. Our hero has a single message that must be kept secret. He has to rely on old technology to make sure the message is safe.

What are the political/social/economic ramifications of the end of digital data encryption? Are there personal ramifications? How can anyone communicate securely?

As extreme weather becomes more and more common, so does technology to control the weather (or the effects of weather). An independent international commission is formed from the remains of humanity to control these technologies so that they cannot be developed into weapons.

What happens if this organization develops aspirations of total worldwide control? Would a single person in the group be able to act against them? How would people fight weather-related weaponry?

The capital is surrounded by security—layers and layers of steel, motion sensors, and automated guns. The capital is sealed in a bubble of protection. It is all monitored by the most intelligent computer ever created. A technician, (who really just carries out the computer's requests), notices a shadow moving in the corner of one of the monitors. The computer has let a spy slip through security, and she is making her way toward the capital.

But why? Has the computer intentionally allowed this security breach?

Glasses, sunglasses, and contacts all contain the technology to analyze things in real life and give the wearer information about them. Some observant people have noticed that the technology has begun to lie about certain things.

What is the tech lying about? What are the reasons? Is the technology becoming self aware? Was the technology hacked? Is this a prank, or are there more sinister motivations behind the deceptions?

A new, cheap, easy desalination device is invented, meaning seawater can easily be made drinkable. A large conglomeration, which controls most of the drinkable water supply, wants to discredit this technology. The scientist responsible for the new device must find a way to get it to the people, knowing that doing so will change the world and put his life in great danger.

What is at stake for our hero if he challenges the conglomeration? Why is his invention so important to him personally? How does he fight something with more manpower and resources?

Nº 82

It's the naissance of cyborg technology. One of the leading companies encourages more people to sign up to be human test subjects. Since the public relations campaign was stunningly successful, the number of applicants is overwhelming.

What are the hidden dangers of the technology? Do the risks outweigh the benefits? Do legislators keep up with the technology? Do they legislate cybernetics in the same fashion as weapons, medicine, or vehicles? How do these changes affect human relationships?

Nº 83

Humanity invents a technology that gives all living things the ability to communicate through human speech.

Now that we can talk to everything in nature, does it change humanity's image of itself in relation to the natural world? If everything from cows to cabbage can form sentences, how does that communication change our daily lives?

Scientists confirm that there is a web, composed primarily of dark matter, that holds galaxies together—the hidden connective tissue of the universe. We discover we can alter this web either by cutting strands or pulling them closer. Our hero is trying to convince both the engineers and government to stop altering the web. He's willing to do anything in his power to stop them.

What are the unintended consequences of manipulating these little-understood forces? Why isn't our hero believed? Is he unreliable? What are his personal experiences manipulating these forces? Has he done so on a smaller scale?

Physical and cyber realities are intermingled to the point that someone's identity online is indistinguishable from their physical identity. Everyone has a chip in their hand that connects them with their cyber identity. If someone's chip is damaged or a virus destroys their online identity, they are effectively invisible, little more than a ghost. A group of people whose chips have been damaged or stolen have to form a society on the margins of civilization.

How do they handle human interaction? How do they handle the absence of everything they've known? How do they transition from living in two worlds to living in only one?

A weapon is created that debilitates the target with euphoria. The weapon is simultaneously appropriated by the military and police forces while also being used as a new drug on the streets. After a successful widespread campaign to get the euphoria weapons off the streets, addicts begin antagonizing the police in order to get shot (and get their fix), creating a new class of criminal junkie. Some people argue the gun is more humane, while others argue that it's simply a new kind of violence.

Where does our hero stand? What is our hero's experience with this weapon? Why does he have a vested interest in its use? What does he stand to lose if it continues being used?

A janitor at a military research facility is faced with crippling financial problems when his wife is diagnosed with a terminal disease. Desperate, he steals a prototype camouflage device that bends light around the wearer, making them effectively invisible. Although his original plan was to sell it, not even the black market would risk such a high profile item.

What does he do with it now? Does he use it to commit crime? Does he travel somewhere dangerous to try to sell it? What does his sick wife think of the measures he's taking to save her life?

A conservationist breaks into the Time Travel Department to try to save a single species before it goes extinct. Time travel is restricted to government-mandated research and observation only, so this intrusion breaks dozens of laws.

Why is this species so important to this character? What species is being saved? What does the conservationist have to do to save it?

No 89

Aliens arrive in Elizabethan times, causing a schism between the church and court. Some believe they're angels, and others claim they're demons.

Where do the aliens stand on this argument? Do some aliens take advantage of the people's beliefs? Do others want to come clean? What happens when religious theories have physical beings to fight over?

ANOTHER TIME

TIME TRAVEL, ALTERNATE HISTORIES

A graduate student conducts a study that searches the Internet for mentions of events before they happen in order to confirm the existence of time travel. The study is mostly a joke, until he actually finds a woman from the future. Once the time traveler realizes that she has been discovered, she must desperately convince the student not to reveal her identity.

What is at stake in revealing the existence of the time traveler? Is the time traveler telling the truth? What are her motives?

The Cold War has driven fears about an atomic attack to full frenzy. Convinced that an attack is coming, the president signs an executive order declaring martial law and establishing towns as independent states so that if one is destroyed the rest will not be handicapped. These new city-states must now learn to be entirely self-sufficient and even cut off communication with other towns until the nuclear threat passes.

How would people cope with learning new skills? Would people follow this order, since it seems temporary, or resist it? Would families move to one area in order to maintain contact?

B efore the fall of Rome, Romans were just beginning to develop steam power. They had a few toys and mechanisms that ran on steam. Write a story about Rome if they had fully developed steam before they were overrun.

What would this power have allowed them to do? How would it have changed history? How would this affect the empire's religion/economy/daily life?

The key to time travel turns out to have nothing to do with technology. Instead, it relies on an act of will and a specific series of thoughts and practices that can be carried out by practically any individual. This discovery is kept secret from the public until it is accidentally leaked. Now, the public is finding that anyone can time travel. The secret is out.

Can a civilization in which everyone can time travel at will survive? Will people get used to this new normal? Will new rules and taboos form around time travel?

Every year, on their eighteenth birthday, a member of the Smith family is hurtled back through time for a year and a day. They have to survive long enough to return home, and not every Smith does.

How does the youngest Smith prepare for this day? What will her parents tell her about what is about to happen? Where does she go?

A single person notices that elements from the past are bleeding through into the present. It starts with small things, the design of cars, wording on signs, and so forth. Soon the differences become bigger and more noticeable.

Who can he tell? What can he do to stop this? How does this change his life/relationships/future?

A cabal of time travelers aims for global and temporal dominance by suppressing the invention of the written word throughout human history, keeping written language for themselves. A small rebel group leaves the cabal to oppose them.

How can the rebels introduce written language to a population that has no such concept? What long-term ramifications are there in a society without the written word? Does oral or visual tradition fill the gap?

A brilliant scientist develops time travel and hides it from the world. He uses the technology to change a single pivotal event in his past in order to improve his life. However, the unstable nature of time means that he must continually travel back to monitor and reinforce the change. He must do this for the rest of his life.

Was the change worth it? Did he make a change that gave him more money? Love? Success? Does he really still have a life to improve if most of his time is spent reinforcing the time change? How does the anxiety of monitoring his past change him?

Time travel has become the new nuclear option. The technology is incredibly rare, complex, and ludicrously expensive to create. World powers race to gain and use the technology for their own national interests, creating a new arms race. Our hero is a spy for an emerging power hell-bent on gaining time travel technology for itself. If he succeeds, it will ensure his nation's place on the world stage. If he fails, his enemies may ensure that he is never even born.

What are the complications of fighting an enemy that, with enough knowledge, can stop your plan even before you know what it is?

We discovered a sunken Greek city that has, apparently, been held in stasis since a catastrophic incident. As it's brought to the surface, the city awakes, along with thousands of its citizens.

How does the world handle these living fossils? What questions of sovereignty must be answered? Do we inflict our modern expectations on a large group of newcomers?

A time-assassin is raised and trained for one task, to go back in time and kill the single person who sets a historical tragedy in motion. Trained and ready, he is sent back. As he stalks his victim he must come to terms with the fact that he can see the target's point of view and, actually, does not disagree with their motives. He also slowly realizes that his entire life has been building to this moment, and he will become obsolete after he succeeds.

Does he carry out his mission anyway? Do those who sent him have any means of tracking him? Does he contact or even aid his target?

MY PLOT IDEAS

_____

_____

_____

_____

_____

_____

_____

_____

_____

_____

_____

_____

_____

_____

_____

_____

100 Prompts for Science Fiction Writers

ABOUT THE AUTHORS

Leslie and Jarod Anderson's work has appeared in world-class speculative publications, including: *Asimov's*, *Strange Horizons*, *Andromeda Spaceways Inflight Magazine*, *Escape Pod*, and *Daily Science Fiction*. They are also the authors of *Inklings: 300 Starts, Plots, and Challenges to Inspire your Horror, Science Fiction, and Fantasy Stories* (CreateSpace, 2013). Leslie's book of speculative poetry, *An Inheritance of Stone*, was published by Alliteration Ink in 2013, and her novel, *The Cricket Prophecies*, was released by Post Mortem Press in 2014. They live in Ohio with a blue-tongued skink named Elizardbeth.